BUT YOU LOOK SO NORMAL…

A true story of living with brain injuries, beating the odds, and finding love.

By: Kara Ellsworth and Chris Russo

First published by Dog Ear Publishing
4010 W. 86th Street, Ste H
Indianapolis, IN 46268
www.dogearpublishing.net

ISBN: 978-1-4575-2075-4

This book is printed on acid-free paper.

Printed in the United States of America

We dedicate this book to our parents Marcia and Kirk and Debbie and Bart. To Kara's brothers Kevin and Brent and to Chris's siblings Theresa, Melody, and Charlie. They stood behind us both, literally, so we wouldn't fall down, and figuratively, so we could achieve anything we wanted to! We would not be where we are today without their love, support, and encouragement in every form. To friends and co-workers who made us laugh and believe in ourselves, and still give us hope for the medical field. A special thank you to Patrick, Sara, and Kay: friends anybody would be honored to have. A big hug goes to all survivors and caregivers of people with brain injuries and for anybody that has been told they "look so normal". Fight every day for your recovery! Finally we dedicate this to each other…

Table of Contents

CHAPTER 1
Riding the Rotisserie

*U*gh. What a day.

I was lying down in my third emergency room in the past 12 hours. What I thought was going to be a promising day that answered medical questions turned into one of the most frustrating, confusing, and life-changing experiences.

Earlier in the day I underwent a procedure called a cerebral angiogram. This is a test where the doctor threads a catheter from the artery in your groin all the way up to your brain. Once inside the brain, the iodine contrast dye is injected and the doctor can see images of the vessels. People usually have this procedure to look for aneurysms, narrowing of arteries that can slow down blood flow, or abnormalities in the blood vessels.

I was having this procedure because I had been having headaches for the past six months along with vision loss. In that time I had lost so much vision that I was considered legally blind, and had talked to a low-vision eye doctor about going to the school for the blind. My ophthalmologist at Kaiser was so concerned about my vision loss that I was referred over to a world renowned neuro-opthalmologist at UC Davis Medical Center. After spending an entire day with me, reviewing my history since birth and doing tests, he had come to the conclusion that I had one of three diseases: multiple sclerosis, Lyme disease, or vasculitis. His bet was on vasculitis. Since vasculitis affects the vessels, a cerebral angiogram would be needed to confirm the diagnosis.

I was actually looking forward to having the angiogram. After six months of not knowing what was causing all my symptoms, this test would hopefully give a name to my disease. The test has risks (<1% chance of causing a stroke), but I was willing to go through them to get a diagnosis and treatment.

I was very relaxed throughout the procedure. The only thing I clearly remember is hearing the doctor comment that she was having a hard time threading the catheter through my artery. It didn't click that might have been a potential problem. I can thank the Ativan and Dilaudid for creating that sense of oblivion.

While I was in the recovery room/post anesthesia care unit I started feeling nauseous. Then I began vomiting. A different kind of headache than my normal ones developed. There was a wave of dizziness and then I couldn't lift or turn my head. I told the nurse all my symptoms and she notified the doctor. I was given some anti-nausea and pain medicine. Although I was symptomatic, I was released from the hospital.

I had an appointment over at UC Davis with a neurologist who had treated vasculitis patients. I wasn't going to miss this appointment. Besides, they wouldn't discharge me if there was a problem…

By the time I was at the appointment I had to be wheeled in because I couldn't walk on my own. I was in the doctor's office waiting for my appointment and got this wave of nausea and dizziness, and I had to lie down immediately. I started sweating profusely and my left leg went numb. I thought I had experienced the numb feeling in the past, but I was wrong. This was numb. By this time my mom was in the room with me, and she quickly got the nurse and the doctor, and they immediately rushed in. The doctor took one look at me and said to dial 911.

I was taken to the UC Davis Medical Center emergency room by ambulance. I have absolutely no memory of that ride at all. The next thing I remember was hearing voices in the emergency room.

I overheard somebody say that I had nuchal rigidity. Nuchal rigidity is when your neck is stiff and you can't move it.

I thought," *I don't have that"*.

I tried to move my neck, but couldn't.

Oh crap. I guess I do have nuchal rigidity.

The next thing I remember, I woke up and there was a paramedic next to me. He asked me how I was feeling, and then told me I was on my way to the Kaiser emergency room in South Sacramento.

The next thing I knew I was lying in a hospital bed. I had no idea where I was, because I couldn't see anything. Talk about confusion. I could hear my dad's voice though. One positive thing with my vision loss was that my sense of hearing and smell improved dramatically.

I was so groggy and out of it. My dad came over with a nurse once they saw that I was awake. Apparently, they said I was going to go home. Dad had said that the emergency room doctor looked at the angiogram and that it was clean. My symptoms were probably a reaction from anxiety about the test. I was so confused that I said. "Okay." I think my dad was so relieved to hear that there wasn't anything seriously wrong on the angiogram that going home sounded like a good idea.

I was wheeled out of the emergency room because I couldn't walk. I was given a prescription for a Phenergan suppository for my nausea and vomiting. I lay down as flat as I could in the back seat of the car, because by now every time I lifted my head I was nauseous and dizzy.

When we finally got home to my parents' house I got on my hands and knees and just crawled in. I guess it didn't really sink in that I was on my hands and knees and couldn't stand up by myself. I guess I just didn't care, either. I just wanted to get inside and lie down.

My mom came running out frantically and couldn't figure out what I was doing out of the hospital. Apparently the doctor in the emergency room had told her that I was going to be admitted. She had gone home to change clothes and make some calls, and was then planning on returning to the hospital. Imagine her surprise when I came crawling up the pathway!

I had crawled into the bathroom in my parents' house and was relieved just to be lying flat again. I vaguely remember arguing with my parents that I was not going back to the emergency room. No way was I going to go back to the hospital. I did not want to move from the floor.

According to my parents the doctors at UC Davis were going to admit me to the hospital. Because I was a

Kaiser patient, they called over to Kaiser and they said not to admit me. Instead I was to be brought over to the Kaiser emergency room by ambulance, and they would go from there. Whatever. I still didn't care or want to move.

I finally got tired of arguing and gave in to going back to the hospital, so off we went to the next Kaiser emergency room in Sacramento. Fortunately, this emergency room was only about five minutes away.

After being slumped over in the wheelchair in the waiting room, I was finally triaged by the nurse. I was lying flat on the bed trying to tune out the bells, beeps, and lights in the emergency room. I heard my mom ask the nurse if I could continue to lie down while we waited for the doctor. The nurse had said it was ok, but that I would have to give the bed up if somebody who was "really sick" came in. Wow. What a caring nurse. I am so glad we work in the same profession.

The doctor came in and immediately said that I was going to be admitted. At this time I was dehydrated and would probably just be in for a day or two to get fluids.

I was then admitted to a general medical surgical floor. I had two other roommates in a two-person room. The next two days were pretty unremarkable. I was just completely flat on the bed. I felt completely helpless. I knew I couldn't see where I was and who was in the room with me because of my visual loss, but this was different. I didn't have a sense of where I was in the room. I couldn't figure it out. I knew I couldn't see, but it was more than that. I didn't really know how to explain to the doctors without sounding like a crazy person.

In fact, I was beginning to think I had gone crazy. I was told that my angiogram came back ok, yet I still had this severe headache that Morphine was "kind of" touching. I was so nauseous and dizzy with any head or body movement. It was not the usual vertigo where the room was spinning, but the vertigo where I was the one doing the spinning. I felt like I was a chicken on a rotisserie that would not stop. Ugh. Please make it stop...

By day three I was still flat on the bed. I was still vomiting with any head motion and obviously not eating or drinking. I still had my headache, and was still spinning on my rotisserie. Because I wasn't doing anything except lying down, I had all that time to just think. Think about what the heck was wrong. Maybe I am crazy. Maybe I really do have every psychological diagnosis there ever was. I sure felt off. My abnormal psychology course that I took in nursing school was coming back to haunt me. Maybe I am a paranoid schizophrenic with hallucinations? Or a multiple personality? Yikes. What is going on with me??

In the afternoon the doctor came in to see me. He was still puzzled as to why I was still symptomatic. That makes two of us. He told me that I was going to have a CT scan of the head to see if they could see anything that might be a reason for the symptoms.

I was taken down to the CT scan by someone I actually knew. I wasn't in much of a talking mood, so I would just smile and answer in really short responses, hoping that he wasn't thinking I was being rude. No matter how awful I felt I was always nice to my caregivers. There's just no excuse for rudeness!

On the way back up to my room I was told that there was a lot of activity by the doctors who were reading my film, and that they would probably be up real soon to discuss the findings.

My doctor in the hospital was back by my bedside within a few minutes.

"Well … we figured out what is causing all your symptoms."

I was then told I'd had a stroke, but that I would recover without any problems.

Oh, thank God, there is something on the scan and I am not crazy.

Oh wait. What did he just say? Did he just say I had a stroke? But I am 27, and I don't want to have had a stroke.

The only thing I could even get out was, "What does that mean?"

I was told that since I was young I would recover well. The neurologist would be by to see me that day, and the physical therapist would also be by that day to start my rehabilitation.

And that was that.

I called my mom and told her that they'd found out the reason for all my symptoms.

"Turns out I had a stroke."

Silence on the other end.

"What?"

Turns out she was pretty stunned, too, and perhaps a little relieved that her daughter was not nuts.

About an hour after discovering I'd had a stroke I was taken to have another scan done to check for any other complications that the stroke might have caused.

The tech was a little stunned when he saw me.

"You are my stroke patient?"

"That would be me." Wow. That sounded funny to say and hear.

Luckily everything on the scan was good. I would not need brain surgery.

That afternoon I was surrounded once again by family and friends, but I could tell the mood was different because now I was a stroke victim and not just suffering from dehydration. Everyone was being positive and trying to cheer me up, but it was a very scary time for everybody. Nobody really knows how you are going to recover from a stroke. It's not like a broken arm where most people recover in the same way. The truth is that everybody with a brain injury recovers in their own way.

That night was particularly bad. I was still flat in bed not really knowing what was in my future. I hadn't talked to the neurologist yet. I had briefly been introduced to the physical therapist, enough to know her name and that rehab was going to start in the morning. I still had a headache, nausea, dizziness, and was still on my rotisserie; not to mention I still couldn't see. I couldn't walk or even sit up. Was this seriously how my life was going to end up?

Physical therapy is tough. You're not doing it correctly if it isn't! But that's ok. I knew going into rehabilitation that the only way I was going to get better was to work really hard In my teens I had spent many years in physical therapy for shoulder injuries, and I was well aware that you get what you put in.

During my first day of rehab I practiced just sitting up for a few seconds at a time. That was it. And that pretty much wiped me out. I was finally starting to understand true fatigue! During my rehab session I was trying to ask the physical therapist if she could fill me in on anything about the stroke. I hadn't seen the neurologist yet and I had so many questions. I didn't get a whole lot of answers, but hopefully the neurologist would be by soon.

He wasn't. He came in to see me two days later. I will never forget hearing what he said to me as he walked into the room.

"I see you have your emesis tub right next to your head. That's never a good sign."

Seriously? Never ever joke about vomiting to a person who is nauseated!

He didn't tell me any new information. He basically reiterated that I'd had a stroke and that I should recover.

Thanks for all the good information. Guess it would be my responsibility to figure out what had happened and what I needed to do to recover. I would learn later that taking charge of my own recovery was probably the best thing I had ever done for myself.

One afternoon I couldn't help but overhear one of my roommates talk to her doctor. The doctor was by her bedside and was telling her that they had found cancer in her breast again. I heard her crying all afternoon and just felt awful for her. See, things weren't so bad for me. My roommate just got news that she had cancer again. I'd survived and now I just had to recover. She might not survive with her cancer. It is all about perspective (things could always be worse).

I ended up staying in the hospital for another week. I continued to work on my physical therapy every day while I was there. I went from just sitting up for a few seconds to dangling my feet on the side of the bed for a few seconds. While I was in bed I would practice walking by moving my feet up and down. Even that felt strange and foreign to me. But, I l kept at it. It's walking, for crying out loud. How hard can it really be? I do this every day without a second thought. Why do I have to really put all my concentration on just moving my right foot and then my left foot? I remember having to actually say the action I wanted to do. "Move right foot. Move left foot."

I was also working on just sitting up. I would start for a few seconds and then start to wobble, and the dizziness would take over, forcing me to be flat again. I kept at it though. I knew I had to push through. I had many internal conversations telling myself to keep at it, work through it.

By the day I was supposed to be discharged I could sit up for a few minutes at a time. It may not sound like a big accomplishment, but I was ecstatic at every little skill I had accomplished. You have to be.

The afternoon came and I was excited and absolutely terrified to be going home. When the nurse came in to go over my discharge instructions they asked if it would be ok if I went home without a walker, because the discharge planner forgot to order one for me.

"Um… I can't balance without a walker, so I need that!"

The next morning I finally had a wonderful nurse. She had floated from another unit, but I remember her because she was awesome and treated me like a person; no snide remarks about how I should be grateful that I was receiving the anti-nausea medicine, Zofran. At the time it was new and very expensive. Since I was receiving the medicine every four hours, I was repeatedly told by a nurse how I ought to be grateful that I was getting this medicine, as it was usually reserved for cancer patients and not just for people who were nauseous.

I was wheeled out of the hospital and "enjoyed" my first car ride home. Thank goodness it was less than five minutes away. My new home apparently meant my old bedroom in my parents' house. I was not sent to a rehab facility, so all of a sudden my parents were forced into the role of being my 24-hour caregivers.

Once I was settled back into my old bedroom I just slept, because I was exhausted. Anyone who has been in the hospital knows how good it feels to be discharged and back in familiar surroundings. Now I felt like I could really concentrate on my recovery.

I was supposed to have physical therapy at home, but I received a call from Kaiser saying that they had cancelled that service because my parents were there, and they could take me to the facility. Of course my parents were more than happy and willing to do whatever it took to help, but a big point of the home rehab was because I had such a hard time with motion, and car rides were definitely now my enemy.

The next day was a big day. I had about a 20-minute car ride to my physical therapy appointment. I remember thinking that the car ride itself was enough therapy for me! I was really hoping that I was going to be working with Janine. She had been my physical therapist for years, and she was amazing. She had worked with me for years with my shoulder injuries. I was not paired up with her, but with another physical therapist, Maureen, that turned out to be great as well. Good thing too, since we were going to be working with each other three times a week.

Car rides took a lot out of me. I would have to be flat in the back seat. I was not vomiting anymore, but was still nauseous. I would suck down Zofran and Valium like it was candy, but I really didn't care.

Since I had stopped vomiting I realized that it had been about two weeks since my angiogram, and I had about a week's worth of vomit in my hair. Ugh. That's just gross. I didn't know how I was going to wash my hair if I could barely lift my head up. I had a shower seat, but I wasn't able to get my hair clean.

My hairdresser, Dee, was fantastic! She had me come over to her shop and she washed my hair in the big wash bins. My hair is really thick, and it took a lot of washings just to get it clean. Even though I was lying flat, I still had to have my head upright a little bit to even fit into the sink. Yikes. I was nauseous and was really spinning on my rotisserie, but it felt good mentally to have clean hair. She washed my hair very gently, knowing that any movement made my head "go". She would end up washing my hair twice a week for the next few months. I was absolutely grateful for her.

The next day I had an appointment with my neurologist. I had been seeing him for the past few months because of my recent bout of headaches. We had a good doctor/patient relationship going, and I was really interested in what he was going to say about this whole situation.

He was located in South Sacramento. That's about a 30-minute car ride from my parents' house, and also the location of where I was discharged after my angiogram, and from the emergency room.

I don't remember how he started the conversation, but it got interesting really fast. He was really upset at what had happened. He said that he had started investigations into what was done to me, but as of today I have never heard what became of those. I don't think he was too impressed that the emergency room doctor had said that my symptoms were due to my stress level about the angiogram. Up until then I did not know the emergency room doctor had thought that. That news made me even more upset.

We had discussed my medications and that I should continue on my Valium and Meclizine for dizziness, Zofran for nausea, and another pain medicine for my headaches. I would also continue to wear the Scopolamine patch for motion sickness. I was not on any blood thinning medications from the stroke, because my stroke was caused by the angiogram. Apparently, during the procedure the catheter went through an artery, causing a bleed which resulted in the stroke.

I would have benefitted from receiving clot busting medicine if it had been given within the first three hours of symptoms.

Now I was finally getting some of my questions answered after a couple of weeks of just anger and confusion.

We were talking more, and he realized that I had never actually seen a picture of my stroke. He brought up the pictures of the CT scan on the computer and I looked at them. I still couldn't see, but I was able to make out a big white spot.

I had lost the entire left part of my cerebellum and a chunk of my right side. Apparently, he was pretty impressed that I was even able to sit up for periods at a time, since the cerebellum is the part of the brain that coordinates movement, balance, and equilibrium. That would explain a lot of my symptoms.

He had asked if I had any trouble swallowing. I could swallow, but I had been having trouble with pills and sometimes with food. I hadn't actually put it together, but it turns out I was very lucky even being able to swallow. Remarkably, the stroke had spared taking out the nerves that control swallowing. On my scan you can see that the stroke went around the major structures involved in swallowing.

I knew that I'd had a stroke, but I just didn't realize how big it was and how much brain I'd really lost. Grrrr......

Here I am flat in the hospital.

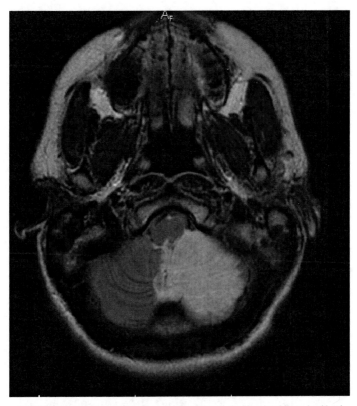

A CT scan of my brain. The white chunk in the bottom half of the scan is the area missing from the stroke.

CHAPTER 2
Chin to Chest

I would like to think I was your ordinary, incredibly sarcastic, 20-year-old guy. I tried to get to the gym every day. I am pretty sure I had the same fears and phobias most people have, but my biggest fear was always to wake up in a hospital. I don't know why, but I just have always had this thing about hospitals since I was a kid. To this day I remember having this reoccurring nightmare about waking up in a hospital bed, tied down, and seeing tubes all over. It also doesn't help that every time I would step foot in a doctor's office or hospital; I would turn white, and get the feeling that I was either going to throw up or pass out. Visiting people in hospitals was always something I loathed.

I had been running a shoe repair shop for a few months for a couple of guys who had bought the place from my father. I have been in the business ever since I could remember, being that I am a third generation cobbler. It was something that I just grew up doing; it was second nature to me.

So there I was trying to get through another day at work, but my head had been killing me. I also had pain in my neck, back, and throat, and it had been getting worse for the past month. I'd been to the doctor twice with no luck of a diagnosis. I thought for sure I had mono, since I had read about the symptoms online when I was trying to figure out what was wrong with me. I thought it might be the "kissing disease," since I had been out with random girls I met in bars. I was a regular in about a dozen bars all around town since I was 17. At the time I was just out having fun.

Another week went by and the symptoms were getting worse. I had gone through another round of antibiotics that obviously wasn't taking care of whatever was wrong with me. I saw another doctor and had my third throat culture. I'm not sure why but I made my sister Theresa come to the appointment, it was a comfort to have her there. This time they also took blood, thank God! Maybe my blood could tell them what was wrong with me. I almost passed out from the blood draw, which was a whopping one vile. I got outside and threw up. This better had been worth it.

The next day I was at work and called my doctor's office to see what the results of the culture and blood work were. What a shock that it was negative for mono! But of course I was instructed to keep taking the Amoxicillin (yea, I get it, keep taking them even if I start feeling better, bla bla bla. I know the drill). I still didn't have any answers, but I had to get back to work.

I was not sure how much longer I could take this pain. I called my brother to see if he could give me some more of his Vicodin. This had been almost a daily ritual for me; it was the only real relief I could get.

All I could think was: *Great, I'm dying and there is no reason or cause for it; awesome.* This was fantastic!

On top of me feeling like I was dying, I couldn't exactly take time off work. The shop was falling apart with the guys who were trying to run the business. I felt like complete crap and had been working 60+ hours a week. It also didn't help that I was the only person who could manage everything. Who knew what would have happened to the shop if I didn't work.

Another week of Vicodin and way too many energy drinks was what I needed in order to get through the pain. I wasn't in the mood to go out as much as I usually did. I was feeling really tired all the time, and I'd had this fever for over two weeks. Not having enough energy or not feeling up to going out to bars was definitely not normal for me.

I made another appointment to see my doctor.

Wow, what a shock. He ordered another throat culture and was thinking MONO AGAIN! Are you kidding me? All I could think at the time was *fine*. You are a doctor. You know what you're talking about. I'll start my fourth round of Amoxicillin. I mean the fourth time is the charm, right?

I drove home and went straight to bed. A few days passed and I decided to go out and ride a friend's motorcycle. I don't know why I didn't grab his helmet, but I didn't really care. I just wanted to get away, even if it was just a quick ride. It felt amazing! It was just the thing I needed to blow off some steam. I love the air in my face. I just feel free of everything. Soon I realized something was wrong with the bike. I was having issues steering it, and now of course the brakes weren't working. Fantastic!

So this is how I die; being an idiot. All I could think of was my mom's reaction when she heard the news of how I died. Great! I tried to slow it down. It just ended up going faster. I tried to think of everything I could do to stop. I attempted to lay it down, but it was too late for that. I hit a center divider. This keeps getting better and better. I was now flying through the air. I literally was feeling my head crumbling into the ground as I landed face first into the street.

I woke up in the hospital. Awesome! One of the things I fear the most had come true.

This must be a nightmare. I heard my mom's voice. I'm sure she was just thrilled that I'd ended up in here because I was on a motorcycle doing one of the things that she had always taught me not to do. I didn't think she was mad at me though. Why not? I would be. I mean, I almost killed myself, right? All I knew was that my head was in excruciating pain and I was unable to tell anybody. I didn't understand why I couldn't talk. Nothing was really working. I saw tubes everywhere, just like in my nightmares as a child. As I lay there the pain got worse and it felt like there was a knife being pushed into my head, and then everything went black.

So now I woke up and somehow I end up at my aunt's house in San Pedro which is seven hours away. I have no idea how I got there, but all I knew was that I was with my grandparents and they didn't seem to be worried about me at all. Also, I didn't hurt anymore. It was not just that. I couldn't feel anything except happiness, and I guess the only way to describe it was just simply a sense of immense tranquility. That and everything was brighter than normal. I had never felt anything like this before. I wasn't going to ask any questions, because this just felt amazing!

Then came the horrible truth. I had to go back now? Back to Sacramento? I ask why I couldn't just stay with my grandparents. My grandparents said it was not my time yet. Time? Time for what? I wanted to stay with them! I started begging them to let me stay, and the only answer I got was that I still had things that I had to do. Things? What things? Why can't I do them here? I remember pleading with them to let me stay and once again, everything went black.

Vacationing in San Pedro just weeks before my illness.

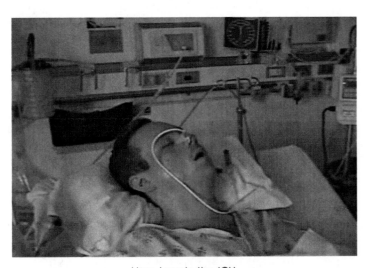

Here I am in the ICU.

CHAPTER 3
Flushing My Brain Down the Toilet

I don't know what possessed me to ask this, but I did.

"What happened to the part of my brain that died? Where did it go?"

I don't know why, but I had this image of chunks of brain floating around my head.

I think that question took my neurologist off guard. Turns out it wasn't anything too exciting. I just flush it out.

Hmmmm.

That gives me a whole new perspective. From now on every time I use the bathroom I will say good-bye to a piece of brain. I can't wait to tell my brothers this one. They will get a kick out of this. Something to laugh about!

Even though I found out information that upset me, I was still relieved to have just gotten some answers. I felt like I had been given the runaround for the past few weeks. Although I was angry, frustrated, and still confused about what had happened to me, I was still really grateful that things could have been worse.

I was incredibly lucky. Not only did I have amazing parents that were always there for me, but I also had my two older brothers who were absolutely wonderful. Brent lives here in Sacramento and Kevin was living in Washington, D.C. Even though they are both grown and very busy, I always either got a call or visit from them every day. You have no idea how much it meant having them in my corner cheering for me. I have always had the most respect for both of my brothers, and getting phone calls or visits was uplifting and motivating.

I wouldn't be where I am today if it wasn't for my family. I could hear them talking on the phone about me and their concerns about my future. Hearing them talk in the beginning days of my recovery at home really helped give me the inspiration to work harder. I needed to work extra hard so they wouldn't worry about me.

Maureen had talked about my rehabilitation plan. In order to help with the daily activities that I was having problems with, she had me see an occupational therapist. There I was able to find some assistive devices that would help tremendously. Two of my favorites were my "reacher" that allowed me to grab items without having to move my head or look up, and the device that allowed me to put on my socks without having to bend down and change positions. Who would have thought about some of the crazy rehab equipment that I got to use? Big kudos to those inventors!

I was progressing well in rehab, but it seemed to take forever. I just couldn't believe how exhausted I was. Maureen would remind me that not only was my brain having to recover from a major injury, but it was also trying to repair itself at the same time. Not a small task, considering how much brain I'd actually lost. I didn't feel so bad about sleeping so much after thinking about it that way! I then started to rethink how I thought about sleeping, and how I now considered it part of my therapy. I was no longer just being lazy and sleeping. Instead, I was actually "rehabbing" my brain during my naps. It's all about perspective.

I began to think about rehab in a whole different way. I needed to work my brain out in order to help rebuild it. Even though each part of the brain is responsible for its own function, the different parts are connected together. So, Maureen was not surprised that I had deficits or changes in other parts of my brain, even though the actual injury was only to the cerebellum. She had explained that when the part of my brain had died the connections to the other parts of the brain died as well. I would need to rebuild those connections. My brain had changed, and I was just going to have to accept that and learn how to deal with the new changes.

In nursing school I'd studied about the anatomy and physiology of strokes, but I really didn't understand the total impact a brain injury can have on your life. Sure I had learned about what parts of the brain did what, and knew that rehab was working on getting those parts back. What I didn't understand was all the emotional and spiritual rehab I would be going through as I repaired my brain.

Early on in my rehab journey I came to realize that I would have to work like I had never worked before. I thought that I had worked hard in the past. I was an athlete that went to college on a swimming scholarship, and thought that I had worked hard. I didn't. I understood that now. I had gotten by on natural talent. Not now. Now I would have to work hard.

About week three into rehab I started thinking that in order for me to be able to keep my head up for periods of time I would have to just do it. No matter how much I was spinning on my rotisserie, I would just sit up and work through it. I started sitting up for a few minutes at a time. Yes I was dizzy, but I would just nap more. After all, napping was part of rehab, too! Pretty soon I was sitting up for not just minutes, but for 30-minute periods. That turned into an hour or so. One of my first victories in rehab was to sit up. Woohoo!

Now that I was able to sit up I could really focus on walking. Even though I could hold my head up, I was still not able to look up when walking. Maybe it was because I was looking at my feet making sure I was stepping with my right foot and then my left. My entire gait had changed. I felt awkward while walking. I didn't have a normal gait. It was a very odd feeling. I had never really thought that much about walking and now every step I took I was focused on just moving my right foot after my left foot. I still had my head down when using my walker, so that made it easier for me to watch my feet and concentrate.

One day my brother Kevin called and announced that he and his girlfriend were getting married. Soon too. Within a month. Holy cow, this was the most exciting and motivating news. I not only had the utmost respect for my brother, but his fiancée Alyssa, too.

They are absolutely amazing. They wanted to have their wedding in Sacramento just so it would be easier on me. That was not going to happen. Alyssa had grown up on the East Coast and they were both now living in D.C. They were going to get married where they wanted. No way was I going to be responsible for their having to get married in Sacramento just for me.

So it was set. They were going to be married at their cabin in the Adirondacks, New York. I had a month to get ready. I wanted to be able to show them that I could walk with my head up at their wedding.

The next time I saw my neurologist he was surprised that I was still in my walker. I was devastated. I thought I was progressing along really well. What was I doing wrong? Does this mean my rehab was not going the way it should? I think this was the first time I had really cried since my stroke. Sure I had times when I would just randomly cry, but this time I was actually thinking the worst, and for the first time felt sorry for myself.

Is this what my future is going to be? Am I only going to be able to sit up for a few hours, spin on my rotisserie, and have my parents drive me around everywhere? A few months ago I was a thriving 26-year-old working full time as a nurse. My future was looking good, and now it wasn't.

My pity party lasted until the next day when I saw my physical therapist. Maureen got through to me that I was actually doing so much better than anyone had thought. Most people didn't even think I would be able to sit up by myself. Doctors may know how to treat the immediate disease, but they may not know how rehabilitation works at all. I felt so much better, and decided to work even harder.

I was going through so much in rehab. I had so many questions and just wanted somebody to talk to.

Even though my friends and family would call or visit, I felt I couldn't talk to anybody about what I was really going through. I mean I didn't want to talk about finding a new soft attachment to cushion my hands while using my walker when my friends were busy going out and doing "normal" things, like dating, getting married, just driving, or working. I was scared out of my mind about what was going to happen to me. Besides the stroke, I still was being worked up for some disease that was taking my eyesight. I'd just decided that I would concentrate on getting better from the stroke. At least I had some control over that. And besides that, I really didn't want people feeling even worse for me.

Even though I was trying to hide my feelings, I think my mom knew, of course. She had tried to find a support group. She had made several calls and finally found a stroke survivor group at UC Davis, so I went to that support group. Everybody there was really nice, but at least 40 years older than me and in completely different stages of their lives. I was a little discouraged, because there just wasn't anything out there for young people with brain injuries. It was at that point I vowed to myself that if I could I would start up some kind of young person brain trauma support group.

Now I was getting ready for the trip to New York! Although I wasn't walking completely on my own, I had taken a step up and was now only using a hemi-walker, which is like having one side of a walker to hold onto. Since I was still on my rotisserie and had problems with car rides, my brother flew us all out first class. He was thinking that I might be able to lie flat and get more comfortable on the ride. Holy cow first class!

Besides my rotisserie I also had some pretty weird spatial issues. The big one being that I couldn't tell where I was in space. I had no idea where I was in a room. For instance, I could be sitting by the door, but my brain would tell me that I was in the middle of the room. Sometimes I am even up on the ceiling. It is a strange feeling when you have to argue with your brain about where you are in a room. On the plane ride I was out on the wing. First class made it so much better though!

Because my vision was still bad, I heard the wedding was absolutely beautiful. They got married in a small intimate ceremony on a hilltop. Nice, simple, elegant, and most importantly no loud music or flashing lights!

For Christmas, Alyssa had given me a beautiful pair of Taryn Rose heels. Even though I wasn't walking on my own yet, she gave them to me as a motivational present. In the past I wore heels all the time. I loved them. These were a fantastic gift, and I would look at them when I was having a bad day. I would tell myself that I would get back to heels.

It is amazing what you find that motivates you when you are sick.

I had discovered who my true friends really were. Some friends disappeared, while others stuck by my side and were really there for me. I became closer than ever to my brothers and my family. They have no idea how much of a positive influence they were on me. I just hope that I can be a positive influence on them, too!

My parents also had gotten a new puppy the year that I got sick. Wilhelm or "Willy" was by my side all the time. Just petting him was very soothing and comforting. He used to sleep on my head, and I would say that he was providing his healing powers to me, or maybe he was exhibiting his dominance. Either way, I will not underestimate the healing power of animals.

I soon discovered that I had a really hard time multi-tasking. Gone were the days of being able to have TV on in the background, read a magazine, and talk to someone at the same time. I quickly began to realize that my brain could only process one thing at a time. I noticed this when I started getting more dizzy spells and headaches when more than one thing was happening. For example, I would get really agitated if I was working on something and someone tried talking to me. I can only handle so much!

My brothers quickly noticed that I would go into these "trances". I wouldn't respond when people were talking to me. They would last seconds to minutes, and then go away. My brain would get overwhelmed or overstimulated, and I would just shut down. I remember at dinner once I did that and when I came back my brothers remarked that I was just "rebooting".

Now I had developed painful deep bruises all over my body. They were most prevalent on the back and front of my legs and arms, but they were also on my stomach. I had gone to my primary care doctor to have him take a look at the bruises and see if he could refer me to a dermatologist to have the bruises biopsied if needed.

My primary care doctor had taken one look at the bruises and immediately got me in to see the dermatologist. I have had a diagnosis of Raynaud's for years. That's where my fingers and toes would turn all kinds of great blue and white colors. People have always made fun of my colored fingers and toes, but I never really thought twice about it. It wasn't until I went to college at the University of New Mexico, and my hands and knuckles would blister and open up, that I knew something might not be right. I ended up seeing a rheumatologist there and he put me on Nifedipine to help open up the circulation in my hands and feet. He thought that I might have some kind of autoimmune condition, but my lab results were not conclusive at the time. He told me that he thought there was something going on, but couldn't diagnose me. I should pay careful attention to any odd symptoms, and especially keep track if I developed an odd rash. I hadn't thought about that conversation until my bruises started showing up. Maybe this had something to do with the cause of my symptoms.

I ended up seeing the dermatologist and was told that there was no reason to do the biopsy. There was no reason to do the biopsy because I was told I got the bruises from bumping into my walker.

Seriously? Are you kidding me?

I went back to my primary care doctor and explained what had happened. He was a bit confused and got me in to see another dermatologist. Boy, was I glad to see her. She was amazing! She carefully examined my bruises and chose "fresh ones" to biopsy. I am actually glad that the other doctor didn't take any biopsies. I don't know that I would have trusted somebody to biopsy the right spot if he didn't think I needed them in the first place.

I will never forget the day I got my biopsy results back.

I had gone in for another follow-up appointment with my neurologist. We were discussing options about how to deal with my vision loss and headaches. The steroid drug Prednisone might be an option, but there were a few more genetic blood tests they wanted to run. Since Prednisone has so many potential side effects we decided not to use it, especially because I still didn't have a definitive diagnosis. Again I was reminded that it couldn't be vasculitis, because my angiogram had come back clean. The plan was to wait for the genetic blood tests to come back, which might be as long as two weeks.

A few hours later I received a phone call from the neurologist.

My biopsy had come back positive for vasculitis.

I played the voicemail message from my neurologist over and over again.

Are you kidding me??

I had a prescription of Prednisone being called in to the pharmacy, and I was being referred over to a rheumatologist.

I was just stunned. My whole family has been told for months that they had no idea what was going on with me. It couldn't possibly be vasculitis...

I wasn't even mad; I was just relieved to have a diagnosis and to be vindicated. I wanted to go back to every doctor that "assured me" that there wasn't anything wrong and show them my biopsy results.

Later that night my family went out to celebrate the good news. The waitress asked what we were celebrating and I told her that I had just found out I had an odd disease that would probably affect the rest of my life.

Um ... congrats to you ...?!

My dog Willy helping me with recovery!

My mom, Kevin, Alyssa, and me

Our trip to the Adirondacks. I am using a hemi-walker.

CHAPTER 4
Waxing and Waning

*A*ll of a sudden I woke up again. *I am in a wheelchair. What is going on? How long have I been here? Oh, my dad is here with me, and that's good.* The big question is: *Where am I and what is going on?* Everything here seemed familiar, but yet so different to me.

I overheard my dad talking on the phone telling somebody that I was in a rehab facility. I had no clue what's going on. I was still so confused. My arms hurt from apparently wheeling myself around in this damn wheelchair. *Why am I in the wheelchair anyway? Why can't I walk? This is terrible!* I was trying to remember how I got there. Was I really in a motorcycle accident? I thought it was just an awful nightmare.

I kept hearing my dad talk to people about meningitis and something called encephalitis. I remembered reading about meningitis in high school on flyers that were hung around the school, but I really had no clue what it was or what it did to you. Maybe I should have read those things or paid more attention in health class!

Apparently, I had been in this rehab facility for almost a month before I snapped out of it and realized what was going on. It was explained to me that I was in the ICU for about a month after this illness really took over my body. I was shocked and felt numb. I couldn't remember any of this. My mom filled me in on what had happened.

This was what happened the morning the illness took over. My mom came into my bedroom and I was staring off into space. My phone, TV and computer were all off, which is not like me. She tried to talk to me, but I had no idea who she was. Then my best friend since childhood, Patrick, walked in and I thought he was there to kill me. My mom took my temperature and it was over 105 degrees. Patrick threw me over his shoulders and carried me to the car since I couldn't walk. I arrived at the Kaiser Roseville emergency room and was put in the back. I stayed there for over 16 hours, as the doctors were waiting for my blood results. Strangely enough they all came back fine. I was going to be discharged. My dad threw a fit and was yelling to anybody who would listen that they should look at my brown urine in my catheter and tell him again that I was ok to go home. One of the emergency room doctors took notice, ordered a spinal tap, and got me into the ICU.

While I was in the ICU my temperature spiked to over 106 degrees. By this time I had slipped in and out of a coma. Finally the spinal tap results came back positive for meningitis and encephalitis. I guess I was sick after all...

No one knows for sure where I contracted my illnesses (perhaps a rare complication from mono). Apparently my strain of illness was pretty rare, because my fluids were sent to the CDC. During my stay in the hospital my family was constantly around me. My sister Theresa always slept in the room with me. There was always someone with me to make sure I didn't pull out my IV or feeding tube (which I still managed to do, and that is why I ended up having to have restraints).

Patrick came every day and would bring with him car, truck, or watch magazines. These are things that we have always been interested in. He would point to a picture and ask if I liked it. He said that I would be able to gesture to him if what he was pointing at was ugly or not. I guess that was just his way of making sure I was still in there somewhere.

My family would also bring in a different watch and a pair of shoes from my collection every day. I am a watch and shoe hound! They would bring in these items hoping I would recognize them and maybe snap out of my coma. The nurses loved my shoe collection, and would ask where I got them.

One day one of the nurses saw my dad about to break down and cry. She told him not to worry, because there was no way I would remember any of it. He said, which he quotes, "But we will remember EVERYTHING," then he got to thinking. My dad knows what a pain in the ass I am, and how I would not have taken anybody's word for how bad I was. My father started taping me after the third day I was in there because he knew that I would have wanted to see for myself, which I did. There were hours and hours of videos.

The first scene of the tape was me in the bed with a feeding tube going through my nose, an IV in my arm, and sensors all over my body (to this day it still feels like I'm watching one of my nightmares). My mom was pleading with me to blink my eyes as I was staring off into oblivion. It wasn't happening; I was like a complete vegetable!

It is so hard to see yourself regress to childlike form and being unable to perform the simplest tasks. Apparently the only thing that I could do was look at my monitor if they asked, and I would glance over to it. I didn't know who anyone was, or really anything at all.

My parents would keep hearing the term "waxing and waning". They didn't really understand at first, but learned very quickly it meant I would constantly get better and then worse. Nobody could tell them anything except that the only thing was to wait for the outcome of my therapy when I was ready for that part of the recovery.

My parents were telling me that it was the scariest time for them because they were on the wrong side of the learning curve. Every day they learned more than they ever wanted to know about brain injuries and brain damage.

Later in my ICU stay, I was given baby toys that had zippers, buttons, and Velcro straps with laces. These were all mind stimulators that they used to see if I could figure out how they worked.

After roughly three weeks in the ICU, I was sent to the regular floor of the hospital for a week, and then I was transferred by ambulance over to Kaiser's world-renowned rehabilitation center in Vallejo, CA, which is about 90 minutes from Sacramento. When they said "rehab," my father looked at the nurse and said, "What? What exactly are you going to rehab?" It was hard to understand that concept when I wasn't even doing anything at all. It didn't make sense that you can rehab a near vegetable.

During the first day at the rehab facility they put me on a table that would slowly rise up and allow me to put pressure on my feet like I was standing up. The theory behind this exercise is to let the brain start to realize that the feet can touch the ground. Because of my injury, I had to start to learn from the beginning. I had to teach my brain to recognize that I have feet and they should be on the ground. Believe it or not, this was exhausting for me!

On day two my dad was taught how to help me begin to regain basic functions, such as getting dressed and eating. I was just like a baby. By nine o'clock I was taken to speech therapy. There were windows on the way where I would be able to see the sunlight shining through. Once I got to therapy I was asked whether it was day or night. I would respond night even though I'd just seen the sun. After that it was break time. Physical therapy followed where I was back on the table. Hand coordination exercises were next, and then a lunch break. After lunch it was occupational therapy where I worked on some more small hand/eye coordination games, along with computer activities. After a small break it was back to physical therapy. Now I would try to strengthen my trunk muscles by sitting up by myself. I was wobbling in every direction, so the therapists had to hold me up.

This same regimen went on for about two months.

A highlight was that my family was able to throw me a 21st birthday party. I don't remember it at all. I was hoping to not remember my 21st birthday party for other reasons. Oh well.

During breaks my dad would take me out to the courtyard to get some sun. I remember very vividly my dad wheeling me outside one day. I asked him why we didn't do that every day. He responded with, "Chris, we have been doing this every day.". I was confused. How come I can't remember doing that? It would take years for me to remember bits and pieces of my rehab. I was taking small baby steps, but I was getting better every day.

I do remember, as I progressed in my rehab, that I was getting better wheeling myself around. I would race this really sweet older lady to the end of a hallway. I won the race, but as embarrassing as it sounds it wasn't by much.

Then one day the unthinkable happened. It was a day I will remember for the rest of my life! I did the usual therapies, but when it was time for the second physical therapy session I was walking; without a walker, without a cane, just me holding onto the arm of my physical therapist! Then she let go…

I was shaking like the first time you ride a bike. I was all on my own! I swear time stood still, and as I looked around most of the other therapists in the room all looked up in awe that I was actually walking.

It wasn't until after I WALKED out of the rehab center that I learned the nurses, doctors, and therapists all "knew" that I would never walk again! Learning that definitely made me count my blessings!

After I was released from the rehab center they set me up with outpatient therapy. It would be the same type of therapies I had at the rehab center, but I finally got to be at home. After spending what seemed like a lifetime in a hospital bed, the thought of being able to sleep in my own bed was simply the most amazing thing ever! During this time I began to remember the dream I had about my grandparents while I was in the ICU. It seemed that I was right next to them but in reality they had both passed away almost exactly one year apart from each other. Some of my family thought that I was going to be the third one to die. To this day I still wonder if it was a dream or if I was really with them.

So a few months later here I am, still recovering and still going to my therapies. One day I was waiting for speech therapy and as I sat there in the waiting room this gorgeous girl walked in and sat down. My dad had driven me that day, and he looked over at me, glanced over to her, and told me that he was going to go get a soda. He said I should go talk to her. I guess he saw the look in my eyes when I first saw her. It took me about a minute to muscle up the courage to go over and talk to her. As I stood up one of the therapist opened the door and said, "Kara, come on back." All I could think was *ahh crap*. I thought I had missed my chance to talk to her. After seeing her, I started to come to my appointments incredibly early just trying to see her again. After a few weeks I started to give up. Don't get me wrong; I still kept an eye out for her, just in case.

I found out that people with brain injuries tend to get depressed, myself included. I don't know why. I mean, I beat the odds. I'm not dead or stuck in a wheelchair. I should be the happiest person on the planet, right? I can't help but think that one of the causes of my depression was people constantly saying to me: "I know what you're going through, because I read all about it." I also heard: "You couldn't have had a brain injury, because you look so normal." You have no idea what I am going through! I can't do half the things I used to be able to do, and the other half I just can't remember.

So I asked my speech therapist, Karen, about the depression and asked her if there was somebody I could talk to about it. She said to me that she had been wondering when and if I would say that. Quite a few of her patients, who have had similar brain injuries like mine, are also being treated for depression. She then told me that it's just something that comes along with brain injuries. She assured me that it was totally normal. She looked in her date book and said that any therapists she would've recommended for me were all on vacation. Then she asked me if I would be interested in going to a group that she put on for young brain injured people instead. She told me about how it might really help me, knowing that there are others like me out there.

Happy 21st Birthday to me!

CHAPTER 5
I'm Back

I consider myself lucky. It only took about six months for a diagnosis for an autoimmune disease. It can take years for some people to get a diagnosis. It can take years because autoimmune diseases are very tricky to diagnose due to their intermittent vague symptoms.

At the time, a diagnosis of vasculitis was pretty rare. I had never even heard of it before the doctor at UC Davis mentioned it. So, of course once I got the diagnosis everybody was searching the internet wanting to know more about it. It turns out there wasn't a whole lot of information out there about it.

Fantastic. I get a disease that nobody really treats or much less knows about.

I found myself explaining to practically everybody what vasculitis is. Why couldn't I get a disease that people have at least heard of? What did this mean for future medical treatment? It sounds terrible, but I was upset that I didn't have a disease that was more well-known, or at least had been in the news.

I soon learned to embrace my special diagnosis. It is fun to be unique. Besides, when I went in for appointments I was now known as the girl with vasculitis who had the stroke. I am not sure that my medical history should be something to be proud of, but whatever. It is now! I might as well make the most of this. Maybe some good will come out of this.

I was feeling pretty good about the way things were going. Rehab was going well, and I now had a confirmed diagnosis. I just needed to concentrate every day on getting my life back together.

By about month six I put the walker, hemi-walker and cane away; I was walking on my own! Holy cow what a feeling! I remember crying and feeling so happy. The happiest I have ever felt. Even though the six months I spent learning to walk by myself may not seem like a lot, it was. Any time you take away something you do daily without hesitation, it makes you appreciate it that much more. I still don't go through a day without feeling grateful for being able to sit up and walk.

I still remember how I learned how to walk again. Rehab really makes a lot of sense when you look back at it. For example, I thought I could go from sitting up to walking without a problem. I didn't realize all the steps involved. I didn't realize I would have to crawl around the floor on all fours like a baby to start walking again. It was kind of ironic. My friend, Sara, had a baby girl Rachel who was learning to crawl at the same time I was. Yay … we both reached the same milestone at the same time! A few years later I was deeply honored when she named another daughter "Kara" after me.

Even though I was walking on my own, I still had to work on a few things. My brothers would joke that I looked a bit like Frankenstein when I walked. I eventually got over that gait when I started feeling more comfortable on my feet. It will emerge every now and again if I am really tired, sick, or sometimes if I am walking down stairs.

Now that I was walking again I was feeling very optimistic. I never thought, *"I can't recover"*. It was just a question of how long it would take me. Now that I was walking and sitting up, I was feeling more confident than ever. Now I just had to concentrate on my eyesight and figuring out this vasculitis thing.

Part of the big problem with my eyesight was that my strabismus had returned. I was 11 months old when I was first diagnosed with strabismus, or being "cross-eyed," and had bifocal eyeglasses. Picture a baby trying to wear bifocals. Ha! Not so much. Although I was at the eye doctor every six months, I didn't have corrective eye surgery until I was 16.

Now I was 26 when all of a sudden my eyes both started turning in and I was losing parts of my peripheral vision. I was still seeing the same ophthalmologist, Dr. Ruben, who originally did my eye surgery. He was the one that got the ball rolling and sent me over to UC Davis for the second opinion. I have always liked him as my doctor, and thought he was so thorough in his exams. Our plan was to eventually have surgery and correct the strabismus again. He didn't want to do the surgery until I had recovered well enough from my stroke and my symptoms were under control.

Apparently the prednisone seemed to be helping my symptoms, because I was scheduled for surgery just about a year into my rehab.

Yes!!

I was so tired of hearing people whisper about me when I was out in public. I could hear them talking about my bruises, my rashes, my walker when I was in one, etc. Even though I couldn't see them, it just made me feel awful. I didn't want to go anywhere for fear of what people would say. At least my eyes were covered up by the dark sunglasses I would wear because I had become so light sensitive. I was hoping this surgery would fix my eyes so at least I could start looking half-human again.

I ended up having a very successful surgery. I believe he worked on almost every eye muscle. The doctor takes measurements of how much to cut and where to reattach the muscles, but you truly don't know how successful the surgery is until you get to the recovery room. In the recovery room is where the surgeon can adjust the stitches if needed. Thank goodness he didn't have to do any adjusting. When I had my original surgery I had some adjusting done while I was recovering. I can still see him actually pulling the thread from my eye.

I couldn't wait until I could start wearing my glasses/contacts after the surgery and finally be able to see. It really sucks not being able to see. The optic neuropathy in my eyes disappeared and my peripheral vision was restored. I had been having bouts of double vision and those even went away too. Even though I had been smelling and hearing like a dog I will take seeing any day.

In my mind I was theorizing that once I was able to see I might have better luck with my balance and coordination. I don't know if I was expecting to be able to dance and run around, but that didn't happen. What I have noticed is that every day presents its own set of challenges for my brain, and some days are better than others. While I still can't dance or run around, I have hope for the future!

For almost a year I had been hearing people whisper about the way I was looking. I couldn't go out in public without hearing some kind of comments. I was very, very relieved to have my eyes looking normal again. I still had scars left on my body and face from the rashes though. A friend had recommended an esthetician, Vera Heris, to see if she could help me. She did! She worked on my face to remove the scars so I could once again look normal. What a difference. I was no longer embarrassed to be out in public again showing my face.

I had been in constant contact with the nurses at work during my recovery. With all the questionable care I have received, my coworkers were amazing. They all restored my faith in the nursing profession. I received so many genuine calls, cards, and visits from my co-workers. I can't say enough good things about them. They had actually chipped in and purchased a few months of dinners for me and my parents. It was the most thoughtful gift. They knew how exhausting rehab was going to be for us, so they figured it was the best way to help.

Almost a year and a half after I first went out on disability because of my vision and headaches, I returned to work part time as a registered nurse for Kaiser. I was an advice nurse that would be triaging patients in all age ranges and health conditions. My mom drove me to work the first day, since I was not driving yet. I was still having problems with my dizziness and spatial issues. I had also sold my car during recovery. What was the point of owning a car if I couldn't see to drive? I was so excited to be back at work. Granted, I only worked four hours a day and took a nap afterwards, but that's ok. I was working, earning a paycheck, and had health insurance again. Having to pay for Cobra every month just sucks.

I was still seeing my physical therapist when I returned to work but now I was down to one visit a week. One day we were talking about how I was adapting to work and if I had noticed any changes with the way I was thinking. I told her that I was noticing changes, even though I couldn't really verbalize what I was having problems with. She suggested I see a speech therapist, even though my speech was perfectly fine. I thought it sounded odd, but I was willing to try it. After all, speech therapists do more than just help people's speech; they can actually help people retrain their brains.

Speech therapy was a little embarrassing and discouraging when I first started. I was working in workbooks for kids in elementary school. Yikes. As I learned in physical therapy, I would have to start at the beginning and build up from there. Good thing I got through that beginning phase pretty quickly. Soon I was playing card games like "Memory" to help build my memory skills, and board games like "Operation" to help build fine motor skills. I used to love the logic puzzles, and was trying to do those. I would get super frustrated at myself because they were so difficult to do now. I discovered quickly that I would have to pace myself.

A few of my favorite "fun facts" that I learned about the brain:

1.) Each minute during a stroke, 1.9 million nerve cells die when it is not treated. This results in the death of 14 billion nerve synapses / nerve junctions.

2.) The oxygen starved brain ages about 3.6 years per hour during a stroke. The average stroke lasts over ten hours.

Yikes!

Those numbers helped to put some things in perspective. One big question I started to really think about was what was my future going to be like.

I had been told by doctors that I would be fine, and would have nothing to worry about in the future. Maybe. Only time will tell. The one thing I knew for sure was that I had a big hole in my head. Do I have a higher chance of developing Alzheimer's or other brain problems because of my injury? What is my risk of developing another stroke?

I was doing so well in my recovery that my brother treated me to a morning of swimming with the dolphins! I have always wanted to do this, and thanks to my Kevin's generosity I was given the opportunity. Holy crap! I was already nauseous and dizzy from the hour drive to the marine park, but my excitement took over from there. Talk about good therapy. The dolphins were so gentle with me. It was almost as if they could sense my head issues. I wasn't able to actually "swim" with them, because the motion of the water was too much for me, but I did get to pet them and do tricks with them, which was an amazing experience that I will never forget. I wasn't even that depressed about not being able to swim. Swimming to me came naturally, and I had always felt so comfortable in the water. I never had imagined not feeling normal in the water. Oh well.

To make me feel better during bad days I made a scrapbook about my journey. It contained pictures of me with family and friends during recovery. It included rehab equipment, doctor's reports, and whatever I felt was meaningful during my journey. I kept pictures of cards, flowers and gifts people had sent. I would look at the book every day. It was a reminder of where I was and how far I had come. Most importantly, it reminded me how much people cared about me and how many people were in my corner. I carried that book with me everywhere. It went to work with me, on trips, on visits with friends, etc.

One gift in particular that I still can't believe is the car that my brother bought for me.

I said it. *My brother bought me a new car.*

I had a brand new Honda CR-V! I never told anybody, but I had to pull over on the way home because I just couldn't stop crying tears of joy, happiness, and pride. I had a newfound sense of freedom and redemption because of my brother's overwhelming generosity! I have the best brothers!!

Day by day I began to gain more confidence as I was driving. Soon I was feeling well enough to even start to think about moving out on my own again. I found a great apartment and moved in. I actually found a way that I could drive from work all the way to my new apartment and not have to switch a single lane once or get on a freeway. How easy is that!? I didn't have to worry about having to turn my head quickly.

On that first night I was in my apartment, I cried tears of joy, and I did the whole next week I think. I couldn't believe that I had made it back to living on my own. I was finally feeling that my life was back on track!

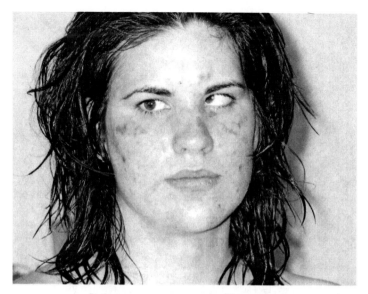

Before eye surgery and with rashes...

What a difference!

Here I am with the fabulous Vera Heris who helped me look
human again! She not only is a world-renowned esthetician,
but also a dear friend to us both!

CHAPTER 6
We Met in Rehab

I was working, driving, and living on my own again. On the outside I appeared to be a fully functioning and normal twenty-something-year-old. In reality I was still in therapy trying to recover on the inside.

I don't care that some doctors may say people can fully recover from a brain injury. It is similar to someone with a bad back. Anyone who has a bad back knows once you've injured your back it will never be the same. The same is true with a brain injury. You can learn to adapt, but your brain will not function the same way again.

Out of the blue I heard about this new group that one of the other speech therapists had started. It was for young people who had suffered traumatic brain injuries.

Are you kidding me? This was what I have been looking for the past few years.

Chris: Karen told me about the people who were in the group and said that there was a girl in it named Kara. I didn't think that it could've been the same girl I had seen that day in the waiting room. To me, the one I saw seemed perfect. I didn't think she could've had anything seriously wrong with her.

53

As usual, I got there a little early. I was taken back to what was almost like a conference room and I sat down. I happened to look up right as she walked in. All I could think was: "I found her!" She sat down across from me and we locked eyes for a split second. Right then I had this feeling come over me that I will never forget. It was that feeling I had when I was with my grandparents; the feeling of pure bliss and happiness. This was strange for me. I generally had not gotten feelings like that when I saw a beautiful woman. When we locked eyes for that split second the only thought in my mind was: "I'm going to marry her." I was 21 years old, and that shouldn't have been the only thing I was thinking. I know it sounds crazy, but I felt complete, like there was something missing in my life and it wasn't anymore. Again, not normal thoughts for a 21-year-old guy. I didn't know what happened to her or how she got there, but what I did know was that to me, she seemed amazing. I listened to her talk about her stroke and what happened to her, and I was just in awe of how stunning she looked after going through all of that!

Toward the end of the group our therapist said we should exchange email addresses. I got home and emailed her right away. I tried not to sound like a crazy person and propose to her in an email a half hour after meeting her, so I kept it simple and just said that it was really nice meeting her and that if she ever wanted to talk or text, here was my cell phone number.

Kara: It was great to meet everyone in the group and be with my "own kind." I felt an instant connection to everyone as we went around the table and introduced ourselves. Even though we all had different stories of brain issues (i.e., injury, illness, tumor, etc.), we were all survivors and we were learning how to rebuild our lives. Everybody there was in the same age category and I felt at ease. This was going to be good.

I was in the group for a few weeks before I met Christopher. It was a great group, but it got even better after he showed up! When we first met we all exchanged emails, and I remember having this strange sense of excitement. Maybe I would even be able to be really good friends with somebody. Hmmm. This sounded promising.

I got the first email a day later. It was from Christopher. I remember him. He had the illness that was missed by the doctors for a long time. He seemed really sweet and interesting so I texted him back.

Minutes later we were talking on the phone.

Even though we ended up talking for a few hours, it seemed like it was just a few minutes. We were instant best friends. It was almost as if we had known each other for years. We skipped the "how old are you" type of basic questions and just immediately started opening up about everything. Of course we had the instant brain injury foundation, and it just grew from there. I felt an inner peace and excitement when I went to sleep that night. I couldn't wait to talk to him again.

Chris: So, the next day I must have checked my email over a dozen times, wishing, hoping, and praying that I would hear from her. That night I was watching TV with my parents. My cell phone had died, so it was charging in my bedroom. I had this feeling I should go check on it, and it happened. I got a text from her. I asked her in a text if I could call her. I did and we were on the phone until around 2:00 a.m. talking about nothing and everything at the same time.

Then the craziest thing happened. Since I had gotten home from the rehab center I had the strangest sleeping habits. I could not for the life of me sleep in past 4:00 a.m. I even tried staying up until one, two or three, and yet I would still wake up at four. The morning after I talked to her, I woke up at eight with that feeling of happiness again. After that I knew I couldn't let her go!

And that is how we met in rehab.

Kara: Good thing I had rollover minutes. We spent a countless number of hours on the phone. I had never felt a connection like this before. It didn't even phase me when I finally learned how "old" he was. I am 8 ½ years older than him. It was odd. I had previously only dated guys that were older than me. Chris seemed much more mature than his age. We talked about anything and everything. Even though we had two different types of injuries, we found some common similarities during our recovery. For example, most foods for a while tasted like rancid oil to him. Food was different for me too. I had to have frozen cokes all the time. We also discovered that we couldn't stop counting things. We would count everything from how many steps we took to the number of cars on the freeway. We counted everything and we still do. When we enter a room or are talking to you we are counting items. Not only do we count, but the final number has to be even. If it is an odd number then we will count again. I also felt relieved to be able to talk to him about how I would either laugh or cry at random times. After a week of talking on the phone we decided that we'd better meet soon. We decided to meet at a local mall. As I drove in my one lane to get to him, butterflies filled my stomach!

Chris: Even though I was back working at the shoe shop, I would call her every chance I got. I couldn't get enough. I wanted to know everything about her. During this I learned that her brothers are awesome. Her oldest brother works in law enforcement and the other brother is a teacher in a high school. I was very impressed and intimidated by both of them. When we finally met at the mall, we walked around holding hands as if we had been together for years. The next day I woke up and had just an uncontrollable feeling that I had to kiss her. That night we had decided to meet up to watch movies. Of course I got lost on the way to her apartment, but it didn't matter. If I ended up in Djibouti, I would still find my way to her.

I got there and we watched a movie and talked some more. When I finally got up to leave, I remember hugging her goodbye. I then said, "Would it be totally inappropriate if I wanted to kiss you right now?"

She replied with a smile and said, " Do you want to?" I then proceeded to go in for the kiss. It was at that moment when I closed my eyes and our lips touched that I literally saw fireworks. I had never felt that sort of thing before in my life. I didn't believe it could happen when I saw it in movies. But it did. That kiss reassured me of every feeling I have had since the day I first laid eyes on her. From that moment on we were inseparable.

Kara: Yes, after that kiss we were together all the time! Good thing, too, because I don't know how we would have paid our enormous phone bills! Since we were together all the time, we started to really pick up on each other's nuances from our injuries. For instance,

Chris noticed that my head and spatial issues really kick in if I am in a car and we do a U-turn, or if we take the on/off ramps onto freeways too quickly. He now doesn't do U-turns and will go as slow as possible on the freeway ramps. How awesome is that!? As we started to spend all this time together we got to know each other's limits. How much could our brains take? We know we will not be going star gazing, going to amusement parks, riding roller coasters, or going on any cruises. We may not even go on any long plane trips. Non-action movies are just fine for us too. We know what our brains can handle and we work from there. We can tell with just one look how our brains are doing and if we need to go home and get some rest.

We even developed nicknames for each other. We call each other "PITA" which stands for "pain in the ass". It is perfect for us. We laugh at our brain injuries. We created a game while we watched the TV show *House*. Every time one of the doctors mentioned one of our "issues," we would take a drink. Between our meningitis, encephalitis, stroke, and vasculitis, we had some good times watching that show. You have to be able to laugh at yourself! Another one of our favorite things to do is listening to Dr. Billy Goldberg and Dr. Ira Breite on XM Radio. We love listening to their shows. It is just a great combination of medicine and humor.

Chris: I have always had a million and half things going through my mind. I still have crazy things going on in there, but now after this injury I have trouble verbally expressing the correct thought. Kara somehow had always known exactly what was going on and has a calming influence on me, which allows me to actually say what I am thinking. Somehow she is patient enough to deal with the word vomit that comes out of my mouth.

Things started looking up for the two of us. I returned to school and was thinking about pursuing a new career. In the process of doing that an opportunity came along for me to own my own shoe repair shop. Being that the business is in my blood, it's something that has always sucked me back in. It felt awkward at first performing the same skills I had been doing since I was 12. Slowly, I began to feel more comfortable. To this day I still have moments when I will be working on something and out of nowhere I'll completely forget what is next in the process. It may take a minute, but I eventually get it.

Kara: We were both doing well after we returned to work. I was thrilled to not only be back helping and advising patients, but making sure that they were receiving the care they needed. Our calls are timed, and we are expected to complete calls within a certain amount of minutes. Since I was taking longer to process, I needed my neurologist to write a note saying I could have extra time to complete my calls. I knew I had a wonderful RN manager before, but after I returned to work I found out just how great she really was. She had fought for me to be able to return to my job. Since my stroke a lot of managers were unsure if I could still actually perform my skills. Patti fought for me to have the opportunity to at least try. After I returned to work I had the best performance reviews. I have always had empathy for patients, but now I know I am a much better nurse.

To enjoy life and really test my brain, my mom and I took a two-week trip to Ireland. It was absolutely amazing! We had a fabulous time touring all of Ireland. It was my first trip oversees. It was a long plane ride sitting on top of the plane and on the wings. I also discovered that

I don't do well even on ships in the water. We were travelling on a barge and maybe ten minutes after we started moving I spent the rest of the ride vomiting in the bathroom. No more boats for me.

We both know our limits, and know when we have to rest before our heads start going crazy. I can usually tell if I am going to have a good or bad day when I first wake up in the morning. If I have a lot of spatial issues, then I know it is not a good day for me to drive or do a whole lot. It may sound silly, but I have learned this through trial and error. I understand that if I don't rest when I start to have symptoms, I may overdo it and wind up lying in bed for a few days, versus taking control of the symptoms when they first appear and maybe only lying in bed for half a day. During this period of adjusting to work I ended up being diagnosed with systemic lupus or SLE. So, I added another medication to the mix and moved forward. I thought I had become light and sun sensitive because of my eye problems and stroke, but maybe it was because of the lupus. Who knows what causes what symptoms anymore? Either way, I now was able to add another disease to our *House* drinking game.

Chris: One night Kara got the brilliant idea to see if she could swim. It was not such a good idea. The motion from the water made her sick. She ended up vomiting, and I was there to clean it up. Before I met her any bodily fluids would have made me nauseous, or worse. As I was taking care of her, I realized that I could do this forever. I proposed to her that night, vomit in her hair and all. I knew that whatever life throws at us, together we can handle it and make it through!

CHAPTER 7
We Might Have a Full Brain Together

*W*e were pretty well known in circles around Kaiser. Several doctors have joked that between my chunk and the pieces gone from his illness that we might have a full brain between us. Yay! I knew there was a reason we are supposed to be together.

The day was finally here.

We got married in a small ceremony in the old mission in Carmel, CA. We had our immediate family with aunts, uncles, and just a few close friends. It was absolutely perfect for us, because we don't do well with crowds, loud music, bright lights or dancing. Exactly what we both wanted! Our family and friends that had been there for us through our recovery were now sharing in our happiness and victory. We are positive that a lot of people didn't think they would see the day either one of us would walk without any assistance down the aisle.

It really didn't feel any different now being a married couple. We already had such an instant connection that it just seemed natural we would get married. It is very comforting to know that your spouse is also your best friend. You've been through many challenging events and have overcome many obstacles. You have heard, seen, and been around them at their worst and best. And now we know we have each other to count on no matter what the future may hold.

We were starting to feel like our lives were returning to a "normal pattern." We were back driving, working in our previous jobs, and looking toward the future. It was quite a change from a few years back. We even bought our first home together. It is not our dream home, but we bought it ourselves, it is comfortable, and it works for us.

Months went by and things were going well. We had both managed to stay out of the hospital and we were functioning like normal people. It was a good sign for us! Things were going so well that I had decided to really challenge myself and go back to school to pursue my master's degree in nursing. It was all on line, so I would be able to study from the comfort of home in my slippers. How hard can that be? I was only working 24 hours a week, so I figured this was doable. The first thing I really noticed was that it was taking me forever to read. No more speed reading for me. I was reading sentences repeatedly. Writing was difficult, but manageable with extra time. Classmates had rallied around me and were supporting me. It felt good to be back studying. After a year I had even managed to achieve high enough grades to be a member of the International Nursing Honor Society.

Then all of a sudden I seemed to hit a wall. My headaches were not under control anymore. I was sleeping more, and having a lot more of my spatial and dizzy issues. I was constantly checking my vision by closing one eye and then the other. I just wanted to make sure the vision was still ok. I started missing some work. I was noticing more of my vasculitis bruising popping up. I was not feeling good at all. Since I was a part-time worker, I had AB22 instead of FMLA to cover my absences. Then one day at work it happened again.

I had just ended a call with a patient and all of a sudden I got a booming headache like I had never had before. It was so painful that it knocked me off my chair to the ground. It only lasted a few seconds, but it was intense. I had reached over to my neighbor and was trying to talk, but I couldn't get anything out. She immediately got the nurse manager and she came over. I tried to tell her what had happened, but it all came out garbled. OMG what was going on? Now I was starting to panic. Within a few minutes I was being wheeled out to an ambulance. I saw the worried looks on the paramedics' faces when she was reciting my history. I was then whisked away and taken to the Kaiser emergency room.

The nurse manager had called Chris, and he flew from work and was at the hospital within twenty minutes. I was lying down in a room waiting for the CT results to come back. The emergency room doctor had said to me that they were going to do a CT just to make sure, but that there was no reason for concern of a stroke because I was still young. I got out, "That's what they said after my first stroke," but I don't think he understood what I said. My speech was still jumbled.

After Chris arrived the doctor came back and said the CT looked fine. Chis remarked, "Fine except for the chunk of brain she's missing from her previous stroke?" The doctor went back and looked at the CT again. I was admitted to the hospital and had an MRI the next morning. No sign of a stroke, but my speech was still garbled. Maybe it was another atypical migraine. I would go back to see my neurologist in a few days to get re-evaluated. Did I mention I was back in a walker because my sense of balance was off again? Grrr…

To this day I have been told by some neurologists that I had another stroke and that it just isn't showing up in the scans, and others are saying that it was an atypical migraine. All I know is that my self-esteem took a horrible blow. I was back in the walker and people could not understand what I was saying. Back to speech therapy I went. I eventually made it back out of the walker within a couple of weeks. My speech problems lasted quite a bit longer.

I obviously was back out of work again for a while, since my speech was impaired. While I was waiting for my doctor to extend my work absence note I had to call into work each day. One day a nurse manager that had not heard my story answered my call. She accused me of being on drugs and that there was no way I was a nurse because my speech was so bad. I was shocked and humiliated. The next blow I had about my speech came when I was calling to talk to my professor about an assignment. I was able to take some time off, but started school up again. I was really struggling. It was taking me over two hours just to type out a simple introductory paragraph about myself. I was having a hard time communicating over the phone with the professor, and she had said that maybe pursuing my masters was not a good idea at the time. I can't believe I gave up, but I did. I don't remember not being able to do something. I realized I needed to just concentrate on getting better at the time.

At this point I had been out of work for over a year. During this time I had been going to speech rehab two to three times per week and working at home daily. Any kind of speech problems will just make you feel isolated. Besides my family and friends all by my side again, I had Christopher, too! I also had the support from the Vasculitis group we go to. What an amazing group to be a part of. I can't explain how nice it is to be able to talk to people in a relaxed social environment. We trade stories, support each other, and have become great friends. Even if I had gotten rude comments from strangers I felt a sense of comfort and strength with their support and love. Luckily my speech problems have pretty much all resolved now. Woohoo. Count this as another victory! Another victory was finding Dr. Jack Rozance, a neurologist at Kaiser that has been absolutely wonderful to me the last few years. Not only do we trust his opinion, but he has restored our faith with the medical community by combining great medicine with compassion.

We are convinced that we can get through anything together. We've defeated the odds before and we can do it again. We've been there for each other through more illness and hospitalizations, deaths and funerals, opening new businesses and losing a job, and just living daily life. Even though we have struggled through up and down frustrations associated with disability we will continue to do what is right. We have witnessed and heard about people who have cheated the system but we won't participate in that. For example, we've received disability payments, had them cut off, and been forced to pay them back. I've lost a job and then health insurance because I wasn't able to be accommodated at work. Despite all the setbacks that come with living with disability we know that we can get through this together.

One of the biggest blows that we had to deal with was learning of my brother Brent's diagnosis of Parkinson's. He was 41 when diagnosed but has been showing signs for a few years. Everyone is having such a hard time with this. This really is not fair. Why do bad things happen to really good people? No one can explain that but we just hope that there are huge advancements in the battle against this awful disease. Despite a pretty average family health history, people can't help but wonder what happened with our genes because we all have very odd health conditions. Whatever the reasoning, my brothers have and will always be my heroes. One thing we can confidently say is that every day is a gift and that you have to live it to the fullest because you really never know what can happen.

Kara "swimming" with the dolphins

The two of us!

Laughing and just having fun together.

Kara's brother, Brent before taking a much needed vacation and traveling the world

Getting ready for the wedding with my best man Patrick

Chris's family at our wedding

Kara's family at our wedding

CHAPTER 8
Guide to Dealing with the Brain Injured

*B*rain injuries are just not cool.

It is an up and down journey through all the stages of illness/ injury, rehabilitation and recovery. Learning to deal with any type of brain injury is tough. People often don't know what to say or do. This is very normal. What we thought we would do is just provide a few tips that might help you with whatever role you find yourself in: caregiver, survivor, friend, medical professional, acquaintance or bystander.

Tip #1: Bless the caregivers!!

We cannot stress this enough! We know firsthand that caregivers are absolute angels. We know how blessed and lucky we are to have had family that was supportive. We also know that we would not be where we are today without them. Whether the caregiver is a spouse, family member or a friend, please treat them well.

This is especially true during the initial stages. Caregivers are the ones that have to deal with the sudden and shocking reality of a brain injury. They are the ones that are talking with the doctors, nurses, therapists, and all the medical professionals. They are the ones that are processing all this new information, and a lot of that information is unknown. There are so many "what ifs." What if they don't come off this ventilator? What if they will never come off this feeding tube? What if they never walk? What if I can't understand their speech? There are no immediate answers to these questions. A doctor can't say in two months they will recover and return to their pre brain-injured self. Not knowing the answers to life-altering questions is simply scary.

Caregivers need to be supported as much as they are supporting the brain injured. It is physically and mentally exhausting. Provide support for them no matter what part of the recovery they are in. It can be something as simple as bringing a change of clothes or a book/movie to the hospital. Maybe even designate one person to be the spokesman for the family so they can provide updates. Perhaps bring some meals over, or even some fresh groceries. Listen to what they need and ask how you can help. It may even be as easy as being a good listener. Give them a break from their sudden life change. It is not just our life that has changed, but theirs, too. Take them to a movie, lunch, comedy show, etc., or simply give them the gift of time to themselves, a "breather." They need it and deserve it.

Tip #2: Every brain injury is different and no two people have the "same recovery course".

There are so many factors that play a role in recovery. Age is a huge factor. We were both extremely lucky to have had our brain injuries when we were still young.

If we had been even 10 years older our odds for a successful recovery would have decreased significantly. Another huge factor is the amount of positive support and encouragement we received from family and friends. Where would we be without them? Don't ever underestimate the importance of a phone call, a card, or a short ten-minute visit. It can mean a world of difference to someone in recovery. Knowing that you have your own cheering section can certainly push you to work harder in rehabilitation.

Brains are complex organs. They are so complex that we don't understand how to even reach our full brain power potential. Don't compare people with brain injuries. It is just not fair. Just because you have all the odds in your favor doesn't guarantee a recovery. The reverse is true. Sometimes you will see people recover when all the odds are against them. There are many stories of triumph and defeat out there. Those stories can be used as motivation, but be very careful about which stories you choose. It is so important to set realistic and obtainable goals. Always remember that everybody heals differently, and don't get discouraged if they haven't reached their goals as fast as another person has. Recovery is not a race. It is an individual process that takes time.

Tip #3: Do not say you know what we are going through.

We each had multiple people tell us they searched our brain injury on the internet, read an article about it, and knew exactly what we were going through and what to expect in the future. Remember, every brain injury is different and no two people will be affected in the same way. However, we all go through our own physical, mental, and spiritual journey.

I will never forget one of the best lessons a nursing professor had drilled into her students. "It is all about empathy." You will never know exactly how a patient feels. Don't attempt to. All it will do is anger the person. You can *empathize,* but not fully understand a person's feelings or symptoms. It is like saying, "I have had a headache before, so I know exactly what a migraine feels like." Unfortunately it doesn't work that way. Even people who have migraines have different symptoms and can be affected differently.

Don't ever try to tell someone with a brain injury that the side effects they deal with daily don't sound so bad. Yes, things CAN always be worse, but don't minimize what we are going through. We have brain missing. This is a life-changing experience.

Tip #4: We don't remember the actual brain injury.

This is meant to comfort the caregivers. Yes, we have pain. We may even have other symptoms like vomiting, weakness, fever, etc., but we don't remember what we go through. We both know that we lived through pain and all of our other symptoms, but we are not really conscious of what is actively going on. Maybe it is a subconscious protective mechanism. We don't know. Please know that while you may see us in the hospital bed and we look awful, we don't remember that. We know we were in pain, but we can't remember exactly how it felt. We slowly start to remember little things here and there, but we don't remember the whole event. It is not like a broken arm. Usually you can remember the whole process of the events surrounding the break. That is not true about us and our brain injuries. We remember little flashes of events.

If you have the means, please take pictures or videos of us during our recovery. It helps us to realize and appreciate how far we've come! We were shocked when we relived some of our videos or saw pictures. That was us? We routinely look at the pictures and videos just to remind us where we were and how far we've come. They are inspirational to us!

Tip #5: We will be different after the injury. Please try to accept that.

It is so hard to overhear people talk about how well we used to be able to do some activity. We've heard that numerous times, too. Please don't talk about how I "used to be" a fantastic natural athlete when I am struggling to even throw a ball. Negatives are so easy to focus on when you are dealing with a serious injury. Trust us; we know. We have been there struggling with the "I can't do this" feeling. It is not easy to be positive when your life has changed so dramatically. It is a huge reality check when you can't do things that you previously took for granted (like walking). It can be so easy to be negative, but we choose to focus on being positive. Every little bit of positive energy helps when you are in recovery. Encourage us, and don't remind us of the things we can't do. We know we can't do them! There is no need to remind us.

We have learned that no matter how well we recover, we are different after a brain injury. We can work as hard as we want, but sometimes there are some skills that we may never be able to regain or be able to adapt to. We can't even begin to express how frustrating it is for us to live like that. We can't even begin to understand how frustrating that is for people who have to deal with our "new" brains! Understandably it is very difficult to cope with our injured brains, but please learn to try to accept and embrace the new us. *Our lives may now be headed in a different direction. A much different one than we originally thought. We are making every effort to cope and make the best of our situation!* We miss our brains too, and we don't want to spend our energy reflecting on how we used to be. We have learned that we can't spend energy thinking about how well we used to be able to do something when sometimes it takes all of our effort just to stand up in a shower!

Tip #6: Recovery is a life-long process. It never ends.

Yes, we may now look normal on the outside, but trust us, there is some crazy stuff going on in our heads sometimes! We work really hard to look normal. It can be tiring just to carry out normal daily activities that we had previously taken for granted. We can't stress enough how our road to recovery has numerous ups and downs. Yes, we have overcome numerous obstacles, but we are still working daily on recovery. It may not be so obvious since you can't see it. You can see that we don't have walkers anymore, but you can't see how we struggle to learn how to process things efficiently and not get overwhelmed by loud sounds, lights, or crowds of people. Trying not to get lost, and sometimes just trying to walk backwards or drive in reverse, can be extremely difficult and takes all our effort.

We think people tend to associate brain injuries with speech problems, walkers, and drooping of the face. Since we don't have any of those we feel our brain injuries and recovery get overlooked and dismissed. Please don't judge us in the ten minutes you meet us. You may think there is nothing wrong with us, but try spending a few hours or even a day and you will see the "little things" we do to adapt to our injuries. We are proud of the physical obstacles we have overcome, but we also want people to recognize the challenges you may not see. As strange as it may sound, we sometimes get our feelings hurt when people say we have completely recovered and they don't acknowledge all the mental challenges we deal with on a daily basis. We can tell you for a fact we process information slower and differently than before. We definitely have memory issues as well. And, like everybody else, it only gets worse when we are tired or sick. We work very hard to look normal. Please just appreciate that fact. When we tell you that we have trouble doing something, don't dismiss what we say. We live our brain injury and we know how it affects us.

Living with a brain injury or taking care of someone who has had one is not an easy process. It is a journey filled with ups, downs, and just about every other emotion in-between. It is a continual process that everybody must work on. Throughout our journey we have felt the agony of illness/injury, the astonishment of losing a basic function and working to regain it, the depression and ecstasy of daily living with a different brain, felt the power of love and support of family and friends, and most of all our individual triumph to regain our life, find love, and live successfully!

We could have easily been defeated by our brain injuries. We could have given up and not worked as hard to regain control over our lives. There were times when both of us felt that our life was going to come down to living at home with our parents, staring at the wall, and living on Social Security disability money. Through perseverance we are happy and proud to say that not only did we do it, but we are living and fighting our brain injuries every day. We fully believe that we have become better people because of what we went through. You never know what life is going to throw at you. Embrace your family, friends, and each other. Please don't ever give up on yourself or anybody else that has had a brain injury. The road to recovery is certainly not easy, but worth it in the end!

Volunteering for the Make-a-Wish Foundation!

Author's Biography

Kara Ellsworth and Chris Russo are living happily together with perhaps a full brain between the two of them in Sacramento, CA. Working as a RN, Kara continues to pursue her goal of helping as many people as she can. Chris is busy working in his shop, establishing himself as the best cobbler in the Sacramento area. In their free time you can find them relaxing, watching movies, traveling in small spurts, and taking care of their small animal sanctuary, which includes two rescue dogs, turtles, eels, and several fish.